Back in Time

Living and Working in Ancient Mesopotamia

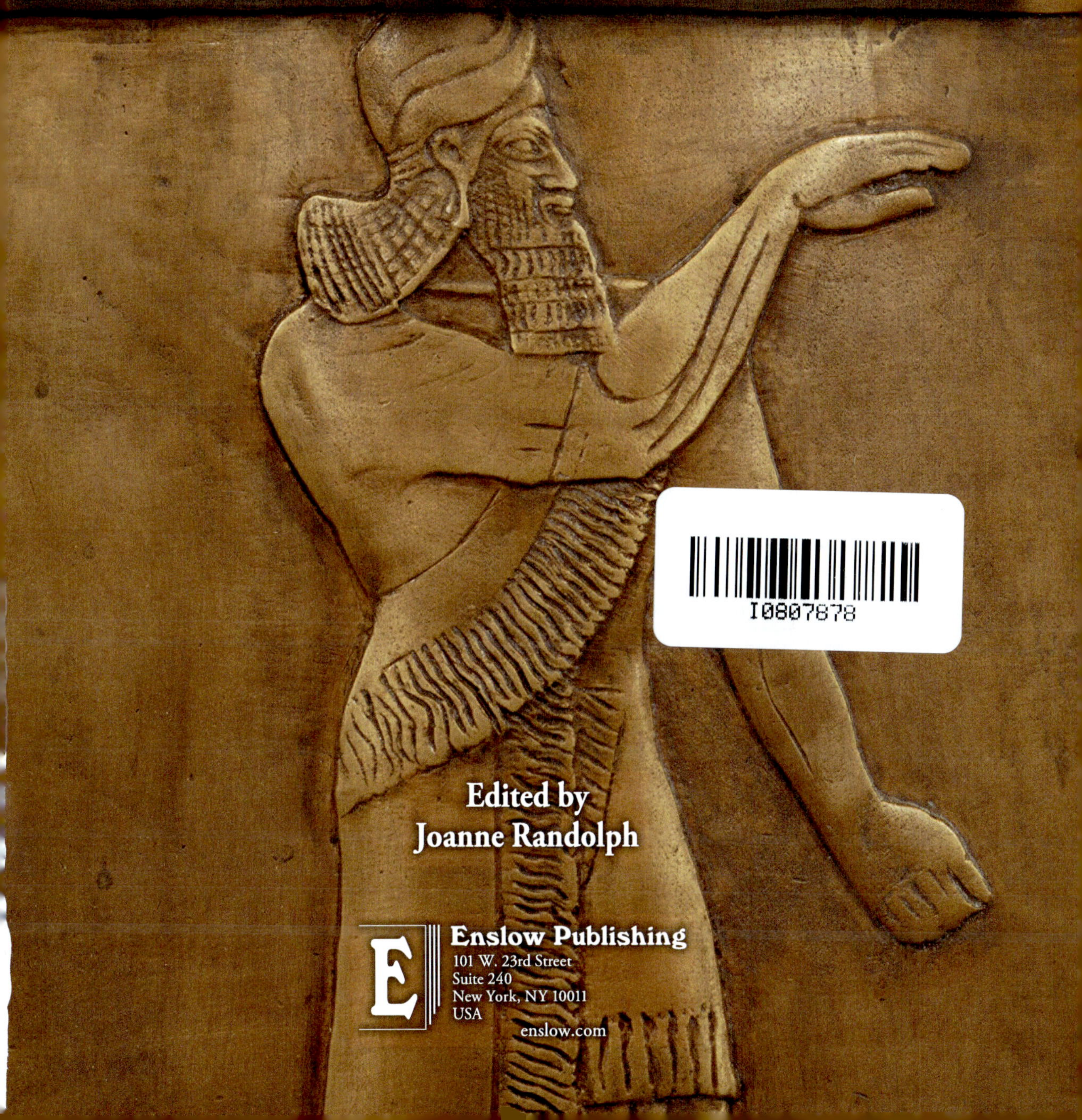

Edited by
Joanne Randolph

Enslow Publishing
101 W. 23rd Street
Suite 240
New York, NY 10011
USA
enslow.com

This edition published in 2018 by:
Enslow Publishing, LLC.
101 W. 23rd Street, Suite 240
New York, NY 10011

Library of Congress Cataloging-in-Publication Data

Names: Randolph, Joanne, editor.
Title: Living and working in ancient Mesopotamia / edited by Joanne Randolph.
Description: New York, NY : Enslow Publishing, 2018. | Series: Back in time | Includes bibliographical references and index.
Identifiers: LCCN 2017001859 | ISBN 9780766089587 (library bound) | ISBN 9780766089600 (pbk. book) | ISBN 9780766089594 (6 pack)
Subjects: LCSH: Iraq—Civilization—To 634—Juvenile literature.
Classification: LCC DS69.5 .L55 2018 | DDC 935—dc23
LC record available at https://lccn.loc.gov/2017001859

Printed in the United States of America

To Our Readers: We have done our best to make sure all website addresses in this book were active and appropriate when we went to press. However, the author and the publisher have no control over and assume no liability for the material available on those websites or on any websites they may link to. Any comments or suggestions can be sent by email to customerservice@enslow.com.

Photo Credits: Cover, p. 1 Buyenlarge/Archive Photos/Getty Images; series logo, jeedlove/Shutterstock.com; back cover, Reinhold Leitner/Shutterstock.com; hourglass on spine, MilaLiu/Shutterstock.com; pp. 4, 10, 19, 25, 34 sondem/Shutterstock.com; p. 5 Universal Images Group/Getty Images; p. 6 Martchan/Shutterstock.com; pp. 7, 13, 41 Universal History Archive/Universal Images Group/Getty Images; pp. 8–9, 21, 30 PHAS/Universal Images Group/Getty Images; p. 11 ullstein bild/Getty Images; pp. 14–15 Heritage Images/Hulton Archive/Getty Images; p. 17 Matjoe/Shutterstock.com; p. 18 Science & Society Picture Library/Getty Images; p. 20 Ashmolean Museum, University of Oxford, UK/Bridgeman Images; p. 22 Werner Forman/Universal Images Group/Getty Images; p. 24 Dorling Kindersley/Getty Images; p. 26 AFP/Getty Images; p. 28 cinoby/E+/Getty Images; p. 33 Mesopotamian/Getty Images; p. 35 Jane Sweeney/Lonely Planet Images/Getty Images; pp. 36, 38 World History Archive/Alamy Stock Photo; p. 42 Baimieng/Shutterstock.com.

Article Credits: Kathiann M. Kowalski, "Ancient Land, Modern Land," *AppleSeeds*; Elizabeth H. Phillips-Hershey, "Land Between the Rivers," *AppleSeeds*; Julie Doyle Durway, "City Life," *AppleSeeds*; Jerry Miller, "Good Eats in Babylon," *AppleSeeds*; Sarah J. Ball, "The Ashipu Will See You Now," *AppleSeeds*; Ann Jordan, "From Agriculture to Ziggurats," *AppleSeeds*; Gloria W. Lannom, "Writing Down the Ages," *AppleSeeds*; Rebecca Wojahn, "Cuneiform—The World's First Writing," *AppleSeeds*; Kathiann M. Kowalski, "The Code of Hammurabi," *AppleSeeds*; "Behind the Scenes with CAAM," *Dig Into History*.

CONTENTS

CHAPTER 1

ANCIENT LAND 4

CHAPTER 2

CITY LIFE IN ANCIENT MESOPOTAMIA 10

CHAPTER 3

THE MANY INVENTIONS OF THE MESOPOTAMIANS 19

CHAPTER 4

WRITING DOWN THE AGES 25

CHAPTER 5

THE STORY TOLD BY ARTIFACTS 34

CHRONOLOGY 44
GLOSSARY 46
FURTHER READING 47
INDEX 48

CHAPTER 1

ANCIENT LAND

Thousands of years ago, something happened along many of the great rivers of the world. People began to settle and farm in the valleys through which the rivers ran. One of the first of these places is the land we call Mesopotamia. The name comes from the Greek language and means "between the rivers."

In Mesopotamia, not one but two great rivers flowed through the land: the Tigris and the Euphrates. Today, those rivers still flow, but the land has a new name. Ancient Mesopotamia covered most of the modern nation of Iraq.

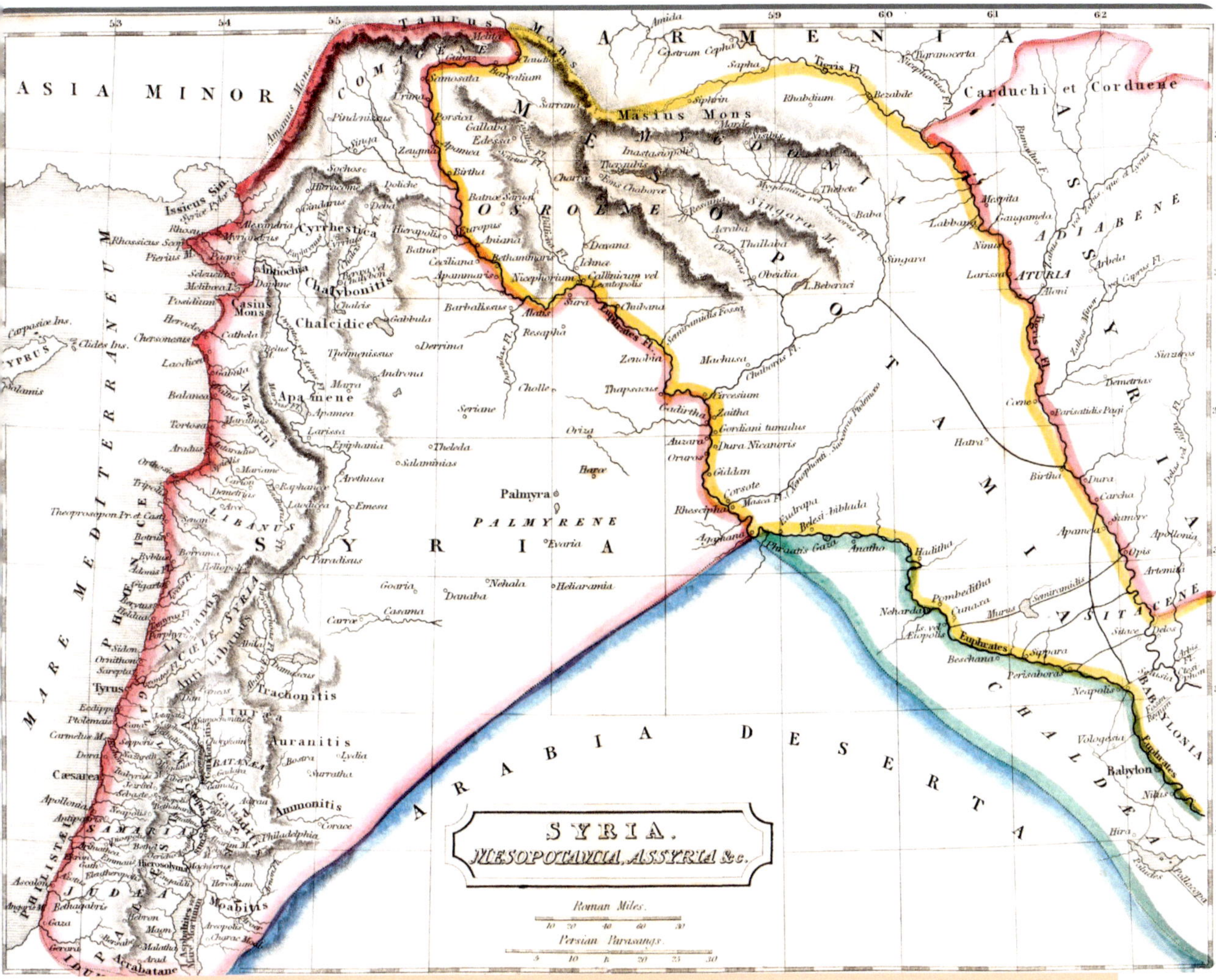

This map shows Syria, Mesopotamia, and Assyria. Mesopotamia is outlined in yellow.

Land Between the Rivers

About seven thousand years ago, on the land that lies between the Tigris and Euphrates rivers, an ancient people gave up their wandering life. They settled down and built homes of mud and reeds. With seeds of wheat and barley they had collected, they began to farm.

The Euphrates is the longest river in western Asia. It is about 1,900 miles (3,000 km) from its source to where it joins with the Tigris.

More and more people gathered in the same area, and the world's first cities developed. We know these people as Mesopotamians.

Why did such important changes take place between the rivers? Like a puzzle, the answer to this question has many connecting parts. Let's piece them together . . .

Each spring, the Tigris and Euphrates rivers flooded their banks. The floodwaters brought food for the soil, making it fertile for planting. But the floods also destroyed homes and fields. Over time, the people learned to control the rivers by building canals to redirect the water. They channeled the water to irrigate their crops during the dry season. These yearly floods gave the Mesopotamians rich farmland. For the first time in history, more food was produced than the people needed for survival.

This carving from the ancient city of Nineveh shows men in the river catching fish in the background and people harvesting crops in the foreground.

This stone dating back to around 3000 BCE has been carved with cuneiform symbols that record food supplies.

Having extra food meant that some people could stop being farmers and learn other trades. Jobs became more specialized. Some people remained farmers, and others became potters, stone carvers, or toolmakers. Some became priests, who ran the temples where Mesopotamians worshipped their gods.

Trade Develops

With extra food, the population grew. As communities grew, so did the need for new materials. Because they had no natural metal or wood, Mesopotamians traded with other people from distant lands. In river boats, they traveled to trade food and wool, and they returned with much-needed resources.

As trade expanded, it became more complicated. Mesopotamians began to keep track of their trades by making marks in tablets of soft clay. Eventually, these marks evolved into cuneiform, an early form of writing. Many of those clay records survived. From them, we have been able to unlock the puzzle of what happened in this land between the rivers.

CHAPTER 2

CITY LIFE IN ANCIENT MESOPOTAMIA

What makes a place a city? Most experts agree that the first cities developed in ancient Mesopotamia about 5,500 years ago. At that time, large numbers of people began living closely together. Unlike the small villages where people had lived for thousands of years, in these new cities, as many as forty thousand people lived together in one area. Often, the first city dwellers built a wall around the temple, palace, and houses that made up their large community.

What if you had grown up in a Mesopotamian city? Perhaps your father was a baker or a barber. Or he might have been a builder, using clay bricks to build houses. He could have been a priest,

This etching shows the city of Babylon, with its tower and protective walls, in ancient Mesopotamia.

studying the stars to try to predict the future. Your mother had a busy life, too, for she was in charge of everything that happened in your house. She also might have had a job as a cook or a weaver—even as a priestess. This was an amazing fact about these new places called cities: people had many different kinds of jobs, unlike country life, where everyone farmed. (Even some farmers lived in the cities. They walked out to their fields every day.)

How you spent your time depended upon whether you were a boy or a girl. Your father's job also mattered. As a boy, you might have worked alongside your father, learning his job so that you could do it when you grew up. Or you might have been sent to learn a different job, perhaps to work with an artist or a musician. If you were a girl, your mother was your teacher. You stayed at home, helping with household tasks and caring for younger children.

SCHOOL LIFE

If you were a boy with wealthy parents, you might have been sent to school. Schools were called tablet houses because the students used clay tablets (slabs) to write on. Beginning at the age of five or six, you would have attended class from sunrise to sunset. You studied math, music, and how to write and read cuneiform.

Teachers were strict and punished any students who misbehaved. You went to school until you were a young man. Then you probably became a scribe, or record-keeper, for the temple or government.

We know something about what school life was like in ancient Mesopotamia because of a story written in cuneiform more than four thousand years ago. From the story, we learn that a day in the life of a student was not so different from a student's life today. (When you read this, try using the word assignment in place of the word tablet.)

> I recited my tablet, ate my lunch, prepared my (new) tablet, wrote it, finished it; then my model tablets were brought to me; and in the afternoon, my exercise tablets were brought to me. When school was dismissed, I went home, entered the house, and found my father sitting there. I explained my exercise tablets to my father, recited my tablet to him, and he was delighted. . . . When I arose early in the morning, I faced my mother and said to her: "Give me my lunch, I want to go to school!" My mother gave me two rolls, and I set out.

Does this all sound familiar to you?

This piece of clay has symbols and a picture of a Sumerian ruler with his sons. Clay was an available resource, so the people of Mesopotamia used it to build, to make tools, and to write on.

Just as it is today, education was very important in ancient Mesopotamia. City life was much more complicated than country life. The large population needed scribes who could keep track of property and trading. Although the king ruled the city, he depended upon the men who worked for him to make sure that laws and rules were enforced. Also, the daily activities of the temple needed to be written down. Educating boys as scribes meant security for the future of the city.

RELIGION AND THE ROLE OF THE KING

Religion was a central part of life. Each city had a special god for whom the citizens built a temple. The temple was the largest and most decorated building within the city walls. Inside the temple, the Mesopotamians placed stone statues of the gods. Priests lived in the

This is the temple of Nin Makh. It was built by King Nebuchadnezzar II in Babylon in the sixth century BCE.

temple to serve and worship the gods. Ordinary people did not go into the temple. They visited and brought offerings to local shrines.

Boy or girl, you would have learned about the role of your king from your parents. Mesopotamians believed that the king was the gods' representative on earth. He and his family and the people who worked for him lived in a royal palace. It was the king's duty to maintain law and order in the city. The king was responsible for defending the city and for taking care of public buildings and waterways. Taxes collected from the citizens paid for these things. With your family, you depended upon the protection and strength of the king.

QUALITY TIME WITH FAMILY AND FRIENDS

Family life was important to the ancient Mesopotamians. The father was the head of the household and expected obedience from his wife and children. However, there were strong bonds of love and affection between parents and their children. Although some wealthy families owned slaves to do housework, in most families the children helped to prepare food, fetch water, and perform other household chores.

You may be wondering whether Mesopotamian children had any time for fun. Just like you, boys and girls had time for play. You might have tossed a ball, spun a top, or jumped rope. You might have played with a toy ship or a doll. And just like children today, you wondered what your life would be like when you grew up.

Good Eats in Babylon

If there had been a fancy restaurant in Babylon, its menu might have read like this:

Starter: Cucumber Slices
Soup of the Day: Pork and Lentil Soup
Main Dishes: Leg of Goat, Roasted Goose with Garlic Sauce, Fish of the Day
Desserts: Plum and Almond Pastry, Fresh Melons

The menu would have offered many other choices, too. The farmlands of Mesopotamia produced a great wealth of food. There were peas, lettuce, and beans. There were herds of cows and goats. There were eggs and apricots, grapes and pistachio nuts, cheese and figs.

As always, poor people did not eat as well as the rich. The most common meal for a worker was probably raw onions, bread, and beer. That doesn't sound like a lip-smacking lunch to us. But the people of Mesopotamia loved their onions, both raw and cooked. They ate other kinds of onions as well. One recipe for meat pie called for onions, leeks, and garlic, plus one more kind of onion! Breath mints, anyone?

They loved their bread, too. A scribe once listed almost three hundred kinds of bread. Most of these were flatbreads, like tortillas or pancakes. Others were baked in loaves. The list included cheese breads, fruit breads, cakes, and pastries.

Most Mesopotamian foods are as familiar to us as bread and onions. But the date syrup they used instead of sugar would seem unusual. And their crispy-cooked locusts would seem very unusual.

They grilled these insects over a fire, then served them on skewers, like shish kebab.

Some experts say that wealthy Mesopotamians ate four times a day. They had breakfast, a snack at lunchtime, dinner, and a snack at bedtime. Poor people may have eaten only breakfast and dinner.

Both poor and rich used meals as a time for visiting with family and friends. Most families gathered once each month for a special offering meal called *kispu*. This meal was served to all the living members of a family—and the spirits of their ancestors, too. Now that's a family dinner!

THE ASHIPU WILL SEE YOU NOW

Getting sick in ancient Mesopotamia wasn't much fun. Mesopotamians believed that their gods caused sickness when

A locust is a particular species of grasshopper that has a swarming phase. Mesopotamians grilled and ate these insects. Many cultures around the world still feature grasshoppers and other insects, which are packed with protein, in their cuisine.

This model of a sheep's liver was used in divination, the practice of looking for signs in the stars or in the organs of sacrificed animals used by priests or seers. Wooden pegs were placed in the holes to help predict what was wrong with an ill person.

people made them angry. A man called an *ashipu* would visit you to decide which god was making you sick. He might try to chase the illness out of your body with spells or charms.

If the ashipu couldn't help you, he could call for an asu. An *asu* was more like the doctors we have today. The asu would give you medicines made from plants and animals.

Of course, you could get treatment only if you had the money to pay for it. Wealthy patients received the best care. Every surgeon knew the penalty if his wealthy patient died: the doctor's hand could be chopped off! But if a slave died, the doctor would simply buy a new slave for the owner. It's surprising anyone wanted to be a doctor at all!

Angry gods, spell casting, and hand chopping: when you think about it, you'd probably rather be a sick kid today than a patient in ancient Mesopotamia. Thank goodness for modern medicine!

CHAPTER 3

THE MANY INVENTIONS OF THE MESOPOTAMIANS

Thousands of years ago, the Mesopotamians made many discoveries that we enjoy today.

Mesopotamians were not the first people to grow their own food but they gave the world new ways to do it. When they settled on the land between the Euphrates and Tigris rivers thousands of years ago, Mesopotamians already knew how to farm. (Before farming, people ate the plants and fruit they found growing.) At first, they dug holes for the seeds with a wooden stick, but that was slow work. By adding a handle to the digging stick, they invented a plow. (A plow is a tool that breaks up soil to prepare it for planting.)

When they learned how to work with metal, Mesopotamians replaced the wooden stick with a metal blade. As the farmer pushed this metal plow, it loosened the soil more easily, cutting a trench for the seeds.

The climate in Mesopotamia is hot and dry all year long. So the farmers needed water for their crops. They created the world's first irrigation system by digging canals that allowed water to flow from the nearby river to the fields. (An irrigation system is a way of supplying water for land and crops.) Later, they built canals for boat travel, connecting one city to another.

This clay picture shows animals hooked up to a plow, a Mesopotamian invention. The picture was made using another Mesopotamian invention, the cylinder seal. Pictures were put on a cylinder and then pressed and rolled onto wet clay.

The plow and irrigation systems allowed farmers to grow more crops. Soon it became difficult for the farmers to keep track of how many animals they owned or how much grain they had grown. They needed to keep records, but they had no writing system. Over many years, using reeds and pieces of soft clay, the Mesopotamians created cuneiform, the world's first writing.

GET ROLLING

Like other ancient peoples, the Mesopotamians made pottery, shaping the natural clay with their hands and baking it in hot ovens to make it hard. Around 5,500 years ago, they discovered that they could make pots more quickly if they turned the lump of clay on a flat round surface—what we now call a pottery wheel.

The invention of the pottery wheel allowed the Mesopotamians to make pottery more quickly. The pots were also more uniform and of better quality.

You can see a wagon on the top row of this mosaic, dating from 2500 BCE.

Can you imagine a world without wheels? Before the Mesopotamian potters, no one had ever used wheels. It was only a matter of time before Mesopotamians went from flat pottery wheels to upright wheels that rolled on the ground. The pots made on the potter's wheel allowed them to store food and water better. They could grind grain into flour on a grinding stone.

Probably the biggest improvement was in transportation, though. Perhaps someone rolled a pottery wheel and realized that a wheel could be used to move a wagon. However it happened, Mesopotamians were the first people in the world to make wooden wheels and place them on the sides of wagons. From then on, they could move heavier loads faster. The wheel plow made it easier for farmers to work the soil. The wheeled cart allowed people to move from one place to another and to trade goods with new markets.

Other Inventions

Mud, or clay, had a big influence on Mesopotamian life. Not only did people write on it and make pots from it, they used it to build homes, palaces, and ziggurats. Ziggurats, found all over Mesopotamia, are huge, pyramid-shaped mud-brick platforms with temples on top.

Did you ever ever wonder why there are sixty seconds in a minute and sixty minutes in an hour? Ask an ancient Mesopotamian . . . if you could. In mathematics, Mesopotamians used a combination of a system of tens (as we do) and a system of sixties. The 60-second minute, the 60-minute hour, and the 360-degree circle all come from ancient Mesopotamia.

Ziggurats were flat-topped pyramids with many stairs to reach the temple at the top.

These amazing ancient people were responsible for many other inventions—too many to mention here. Just remember, the next time you ride a bike or write a note to your friends, thank the Mesopotamians. They thought of it first!

CHAPTER 4

WRITING DOWN THE AGES

Imagine what life was like before writing was invented. No books, no comics, no cereal boxes to read! Imagine walking through a grocery store with no writing in it. How would you find what you wanted? How would the store keep track of what it had or what it needed to order?

Early humans used their hands and spoken words to communicate with each other. Those ways are great, but leave no record. They are used in a moment, then the message vanishes forever. Speech and gestures probably worked fine, however, until people began to need some way to keep track of what they were doing.

Ancient humans began drawing pictures on rocks and cave walls more than twenty-five thousand years ago. We don't know exactly how or when this began—maybe people picked up sharp rocks and scratched on the cave walls, or maybe they used the blackened end of burnt sticks to draw lines on rocks. However it happened, these were the first steps on the path toward writing.

Those pictures and symbols made by ancient people are beautiful but mysterious. What do the animals, handprints, and polka dots mean? We don't know because we don't understand the "language" they were written in.

For many thousands of years, humans wandered from place to place, hunting animals and gathering plants for their food. About

The paintings in the Lascaux caves in France date back to more than seventeen thousand years ago.

ten thousand years ago, they began to learn how to farm. This meant they stayed in one place all year round. People raised animals and grew crops. Villages grew. And they began to trade with each other. From this new life grew a new need: the need to keep records. But how could people keep records without writing?

The world's first written language began in Mesopotamia (the ancient land that became Iraq in modern times). For the first time, people began to keep track of what they owned and what they traded. Mesopotamians used a special tool to make wedge-shaped marks in soft clay. Today we call this writing system cuneiform. There are many hundreds of cuneiform symbols.

We'll talk more about this in the next section.

Not long after cuneiform was developed, the ancient Egyptians created a beautiful system of hieroglyphics, a form of writing with pictures. In Mexico and Central America, the Maya also developed hieroglyphics. All over the ancient world, people were beginning to write—and there was no stopping them.

An important step in the development of writing was the creation of an alphabet. Unlike picture writing, each symbol (letter) in an alphabet represents a sound. Alphabets have a certain order to them, too, like our ABCs. The first true alphabet came from Greece. Many other cultures borrowed the idea of the Greek alphabet and developed their own.

Through the ages, humans have used bird feathers, sticks, brushes, and more to write on cave walls, silk cloth, animal skins, and paper. We have made ink from soot, blood, berries, and minerals. We use writing to record everything from birthdays to instructions on how to build a rocket. Through the written word, we learn and share information about everything on the planet.

This painting from the Temple of Hatshepsut has hieroglyphics surrounding the picture of the falcon-headed god of the sky, Horus, with a pharaoh.

In the late 1900s, the computer became the most important writing tool on Earth. Today, millions of people around the world use computers every day. We can write, print, and send our words all around the world in a matter of seconds. From the gestures, words, and drawings of prehistoric people through hieroglyphics, alphabets, printing presses, and computers, we have reached a time when we can send the written word instantly to anywhere on Earth, and beyond!

Focus on Cuneiform

Today, we know a lot about life in ancient Mesopotamia. But how do we know? Where did all our information come from? Much of what we know comes from reading what Mesopotamians wrote thousands of years ago.

The Mesopotamians were the first people in history to create a written language. To keep track of trade deals, Mesopotamians started drawing pictures, or pictographs, of what they had traded. They made the drawings on small stones or balls of clay. If someone traded three cows, for example, he drew three small cow heads on a piece of clay. As time passed, people realized they could draw one picture for the thing that was traded—cows, in this case—and another picture for the number. Over time, those pictures changed.

As more time passed, early Mesopotamian writers began to make new symbols that were easier and faster to make than the pictographs. Gradually, also, symbols came to stand for sounds or syllables instead of whole words. And instead of writing on clay balls, they started writing on flat tablets of soft clay using a sharpened reed (a kind of plant). The tablets were usually about the size of an adult hand. The marks writers made were wedge-shaped, giving us the word cuneiform [kyoo-NAY-a-form] (Cuneus is the Latin word for "wedge.")

Most Mesopotamian citizens could not read or write. Reading and writing were special jobs, done by men called scribes. Beginning when they were boys, scribes went to school to learn and practice the more than two thousand cuneiform symbols. As they learned to write, the scribes also learned about other things. They made lists of plant and animal names, did math, copied stories and poems, and learned the laws of their land.

For more than three thousand years, Mesopotamians used cuneiform. Then, as the Mesopotamian world changed, the writing changed, too. People forgot how to write in

This stele, a stone slab with an inscription, from Babylonia in Mesopotamia is covered in cuneiform characters.

cuneiform. After a while, no one knew that cuneiform had even existed. People who saw the wedge-shaped marks had no idea that they were a written language. One person said that the marks were just tracks made by a bird walking on wet clay!

About three hundred years ago, travelers began to suspect that the marks were really a written language. Archaeologists and others began to try to solve the mystery. In 1835, an English army officer named Henry Rawlinson became the first person to "break the code" and figure out how to read cuneiform.

Historians and archaeologists can read the story of the past on the half a million cuneiform tablets that have been found. Without this written record, we would know little about "the land between the rivers."

THE CODE OF HAMMURABI

Almost four thousand years ago, King Hammurabi ruled the kingdom of Babylon, a part of Mesopotamia. He gave the world one of its oldest sets of laws. Thanks to the Mesopotamian writing system, archaeologists have been able to study these laws!

Archaeologists found the Code (collection of laws) of Hammurabi carved on a black stone slab. Long ago, the stone stood in a public place. The Code said anyone who "was wronged" should stand before this stone and ask that it be read aloud, in order to know the law. (Most Mesopotamians could not read.)

There were 282 laws in the Code. Today, many of them seem harsh. "An eye for an eye" was the rule of the day. People who hurt others could expect the same fate—or worse. But many other laws were less harsh. The Code of Hammurabi also spelled out family members' rights and the rules for business.

Laws help civilizations run well. Read these rules from Hammurabi's Code below.

- If anyone committing a robbery and is caught, then he shall be put to death.
- If anyone opens his ditches to water his crop, but is careless, and the water floods the field of his neighbor, then he shall pay his neighbor grain for his loss.
- If anyone hands over his garden to a gardener to work, the gardener shall pay to its owner two-thirds of the produce of the garden, for so long as he has it in possession, and the other third shall he keep.
- If a son strikes his father, his hand shall be cut off.
- If a man put out the eye of another man, his eye shall be put out.
- If a builder builds a house for someone and does not construct it properly, and the house which he built falls in and kills its owner, then that builder shall be put to death.
- If a man adopts a child and brings him up, this grown child cannot be demanded back again.
- If a man destroys the eye of another man, they shall destroy his eye. If one breaks a man's bone, they shall break his bone. If one destroys the eye of a freeman or break the bone of a freeman he shall pay one gold mina. If one destroys the eye of a man's slave or break a bone of a man's slave he shall pay one-half his price.

How did they protect society or make people's lives easier? How do they compare with today's laws? If you had to come up with new laws, what would they be and how would they help people live better?

This column is covered in Hammurabi's Code, a system of laws put into place by Hammurabi, the king of Babylon, around 1750 BCE.

CHAPTER 5

THE STORY TOLD BY ARTIFACTS

In the 1920s, British archaeologist Sir Leonard Woolley led an archaeological expedition at Ur that had been organized jointly by the British Museum and the Penn Museum, called Center for the Analysis of Archaeological Materials (CAAM). Located along the Euphrates River, in what is present-day southern Iraq, Ur had once been a very important city. Occupied from around 5500 to 400 BCE, it is best known for its amazing third-millennium BCE Royal Cemetery. Although excavations ended decades ago, the research on the finds continues.

Among the artifacts uncovered was an axe. Originally, it had had a wooden handle, but, over time, its metal axehead began to corrode. This metal corrosion gradually spread over the entire artifact. Even the axe's wooden handle came to be covered with metal corrosion. While the wood did not survive, we can still see its traces, called pseudomorphs. This corrosion did have one positive effect—it filled in the plant cells and actually preserved their structures. CAAM's researchers used a high-powered microscope to look more closely at

This is the Royal Cemetery at Ur. There are around two thousand burials at the site, including sixteen tombs that were determined to be royal tombs based on their size and what was included in the tombs with the bodies.

the cells, and their findings suggest that the axe handle was made from Syrian ash. Ash is a species of tree that produces strong wood with good shock-resistance. Because of these properties, many axe handles today are still made from ash.

A Call to Archaeobotanists

The researchers who identified the wood species were archaeobotanists Naomi Miller and Chantel White. But just what exactly do archaeobotanists do? The clue to the answer lies in the word used to describe them: archaio is Greek for "ancient," and botane is Greek for "plant."

Plants were used as food, medicine, cloth, and tools in the ancient world. Sometimes, traces of preserved plants are found at archaeological sites. Such finds are known as ecofacts.

Archaeobotanists carefully extract these ecofacts and take them back to

This is a Sumerian copper axe with gold banding. The wooden handle is a reproduction. The original would have been covered in a red pigment. The soldiers of Ur carried axes like this one.

the lab where they can be examined under a microscope. When seeds are found among the ecofacts, archaeobotanists compare them to modern seeds to identify the ancient plant of origin. When wood is found, the species can be identified by studying the unique cells that make up the wood's tree rings.

Questions for Archaeometallurgists

But what about the axehead itself? Who can tell us more about it? Well, that's the job of archaeometallurgists. These scientists study ancient metals and try to figure out how and where excavated metal was produced and how the objects were made. Archaeometallurgist Moritz Jansen uses a variety of scientific techniques to understand the structure of an object and the chemical composition of the metal. For example, X-radiography can help scientists look under the surface of a corroded artifact.

This imaging technique is also non-invasive—that is, it does no harm to the object. It gathers its information by using the differences in the way X-rays are absorbed to detect variation in the structure of the object. So, just as doctors look at bone X-rays to determine whether a person has suffered a fracture, so archaeologists look at objects to understand their internal structure.

The metal used to make the axehead was identified as a copper alloy. However, ancient Ur was particularly known for its silver and gold metal objects. If archaeometallurgists want to know the region from which the gold originated, they look to the dirt particles found within the object. For example, some dirt comes from rivers where the gold was panned in ancient times. When the gold objects were created, tiny dirt particles were partly melted and contaminated the gold. By identifying the specific dirt fingerprint, we can reconstruct trade routes and figure out the source of the gold.

Perhaps the best loved of the objects found at Ur are tiny gold animals that once belonged to a fancy set of jewelry fashioned for the queen buried in the royal tombs there. A quick look at the little pendants suggests that they are solid gold, but, in fact, they are not. Each was made using a thin sheet of gold that was pressed over a core of bitumen, a sticky but hard form of asphalt. Figuring out the composition of these pendants was easy; the more difficult question was: what animals do they represent?

This golden amulet featuring two antelopes belonged to Queen Puabi of Ur.

A Need for Zooarchaeologists

Katherine Moore, a zooarchaeologist, took a close look at the features of the tiny animals and then compared them with the features of living animals. It is the job of zooarchaeologists to study both animal bones found at archaeological sites and the various ways people have used and thought about animals. Some of the animals represented—gazelles, for example—are easy to identify.

The ancient people of Mesopotamia might have seen deer in the marshy area along the river, but such sightings would have been rare. As for the bull? Well, they pictured some wearing a false beard. What story does this odd combination tell? It may be that, when included in a royal tomb, a bull with a beard represented the sun-god figure and offered an important message about life.

At Ur, representations of animals were also made out of clay, including little pigs. Archaeologists have found a great quantity of clay around the site, as it was constantly being deposited there during the frequent flooding of the Euphrates River.

Clay, which becomes ceramic when fired, is a readily available raw material that could easily be shaped in various ways to make pots, bricks, drain pipes, tablets, tools, jewelry, and small objects such as incense burners, figurines, children's toys, and rattles. Rattles? Yes! We are still not quite sure how these rattles were used. They may have been musical instruments. They were hollow, and one little pig, for example, produces a sound when shaken. A radiographic image of this ceramic pig shows that the sound it makes when shaken is due to three small clay balls moving about inside its body.

CALL IN THE CERAMIC EXPERTS

Of all the ceramic objects found on archaeological sites, pots of different shapes and sizes are the most abundant. These vessels were used as containers for storage, transport, and food preparation. While they break easily, their fragments, known as sherds, last for thousands of years and are packed with information just waiting to be discovered.

Where pots were made is a very important question for archaeologists. Most of those excavated at Ur were probably produced by local potters. Some, however, may have been transported and brought from other places, both near and far.

To figure out where the objects were made, ceramic experts—Marie-Claude Boileau among them—rely on an analytical technique called "ceramic petrography." It uses a special type of microscope to examine the mineral composition of thin sections of ceramics. This method can be described as one that "fingerprints" ceramic objects. By matching the mineral and rock fragments in the clay to specific geological areas, it can identify the area where a ceramic object was made. Using this data, we can study trade and contact between groups of people.

WHOSE BONES? ASK THE PHYSICAL ANTHROPOLOGISTS

Perhaps you are now wondering about the people who lived and were buried at ancient Ur. Human skeletons offer us many clues about the lives of peoples who lived in the distant past. At Ur, people were buried in a way that made them look as if they were sleeping. They had been positioned on their backs with their hands on their chests or lying on their sides, all curled up in a small ball.

This is a skull from a woman buried with jewelry on at the Royal Cemetery in Ur. Her bones date to 3800 BCE.

When skeletal remains are brought to the lab, physical anthropologist Janet Monge and her colleagues go to work. An analysis of excavated bones and teeth offers clues to the age of a person and to whether the skeleton is that of a male or female. Physical anthropologists can sometimes even tell the kind of work a person did when alive and even if a person suffered from any diseases.

Teeth hold important information about a person's life, such as his or her diet and age. Anthropologists examine the teeth of old remains to find out more about ancient civilizations.

Teeth are especially revealing. They can offer clues that will lead to figuring out the kinds of foods people in the past chewed. At Ur, people wore their teeth down flat, almost to the roots if they lived fifty or more years. We know that the foods they ate everyday were full of grit, particularly wheat that was ground into flour for bread. As it was similar to sandpaper, it wore away the projections, or cusps, on the teeth.

Teeth offer many clues as to the age of a person at the time of death. Children have teeth that are replaced, beginning with a full set of baby teeth that emerges by the age of two and then begins to fall out by the age of six. New adult teeth come in up to about twenty or so years of age. Analysis of one skeleton uncovered at Ur revealed that the person died just as her last adult tooth was forming. She would have been about eighteen years of age.

AMAZING CIVILIZATION

We are lucky that the Mesopotamian civilization left so many beautiful artifacts behind. If they hadn't built cities and began writing on clay tablets, so much of our ancient past would be lost to us. Everything we learn about the past helps us understand the achievements and failures of those who have gone before us. Hopefully, this knowledge will help us shape a better future as well.

CHRONOLOGY

5000 BCE People settle along the Tigris and Euphrates rivers, forming the first towns and cities. They begin farming. We call them the Sumer people or the Mesopotamians.

4000 BCE The Sumer establish powerful city-states building large ziggurats at the center of their cities as temples to their gods.

3300 BCE The Mesopotamians establish the first writing system. They use pictures for words and inscribe them on clay tablets.

c. 3200 BCE The Mesopotamians begin to use wheels.

3000 BCE The Mesopotamians start using a system of mathematics that is based around the number 60.

2700 BCE The famous Sumerian King Gilgamesh rules the city-state of Ur.

2400 BCE The Sumerian language is replaced by the Akkadian language as the primary spoken language in Mesopotamia.

2330 BCE Sargon I of the Akkadians conquers most of the Sumerian city states and creates the world's first empire, the Akkadian Empire.

2100 BCE The Akkadian Empire crumbles and the Sumerians once again gain power. The city of Ur is rebuilt.

1900 BCE The Assyrians rise to power in northern Mesopotamia.

1792 BCE Hammurabi becomes king of Babylon. He establishes the Code of Hammurabi and Babylon soon takes over much of Mesopotamia.

1750 BCE Hammurabi dies and the First Babylonian Empire begins to fall apart.

1360 BCE–333 BCE Power changes hands many times as different groups struggle for control of the area. Eventually the Greeks conquer the region.

GLOSSARY

alloy A mixture of two or more metals. Bronze, for example, is an alloy of copper and tin.

ancestor A person from whom someone is descended, typically from long ago.

archaeologist A scientists who studies the lives and customs of ancient people by digging up and studying bones and artifacts.

corrode Slowly destroy by a chemical action.

excavation The act of digging up a site for archaeologic study.

fertile Able to produce abundant crops.

hieroglyphics Symbols used in Egyptian writing to represent words and ideas.

irrigate Supply water to crops through the use of channels or other man-made tools.

population The number of people living in an area.

religion A system of beliefs and rituals used to worship a god or gods.

resources Available supplies.

scribe A person who knows how to read and write and keeps records.

shrine A special place where a god was honored.

symbol Something that stands for something else.

tablet A block or slab of clay.

temple A building where people gather to worship their god or gods.

FURTHER READING

Books

Head, Tom. *Ancient Mesopotamia*. Minneapolis, MN: Essential Library, 2015.

Krasner, Barbara. *Ancient Mesopotamian Culture*. New York, NY: Rosen Young Adult, 2016.

Krasner, Barbara. *Ancient Mesopotamian Daily Life*. New York, NY: Rosen Young Adult, 2016.

Nardo, Don. *Life in Ancient Mesopotamia*. San Diego, CA: ReferencePoint Press, 2013.

Orr, Tamra. *Mesopotamia*. Kennett Square, PA: Purple Toad Publishing, 2015.

Websites

The British Museum

www.mesopotamia.co.uk/menu.html

Dive deeper into the geography, mythology, and history of Assyria, Babylonia, and Sumer.

DK Find Out!

www.dkfindout.com/us/history/mesopotamia/

Discover more about Babylon, its monuments, early laws, and Mesopotamian gods.

The Oriental Institute Museum of the University of Chicago

mesopotamia.lib.uchicago.edu/mesopotamialife/index.php

Learn more about the culture of ancient Mesopotamia, including its achievements in literature, science, mathematics, and art.

INDEX

A
alphabets, 27
archaeobotanists, 36–37
archaeometallurgists, 37–38
ashipu, 17–18
asu, 18

B
Babylon, 16–17, 31
"between the rivers," 4
Boileau, Marie-Claude, 40

C
"ceramic petrography," 40
cities, 10–12
cuneiform, 9, 12, 21, 27, 29–31

E
Euphrates, 4, 5, 6, 19, 34, 39

F
family life, 15
farming, 19–21
food, 16–17

H
Hammurabi, Code of, 31–33
hieroglyphics, 27, 29

I
illness, treating, 17–18
irrigation systems, 20

J
Jansen, Moritz, 37

K
kings, 14–15
kispu, 17

M
Miller, Naomi, 36
Monge, Janet, 42
Moore, Katherine, 39

P
physical anthropologists, 40–43
plow, invention of, 19–20
pottery, 21
pottery wheel, invention of, 21

R
Rawlinson, Henry, 31
religion, 14–15

S
schools, 12–14
scribes, 12, 13, 14, 30

T
Tigris, 4, 5, 6, 19
time keeping, 23
trade, 9

U
Ur (Iraq), 34–43

W
wheel, invention of, 21
White, Chantel, 36
Woolley, Leonard, 34
writing, invention of, 25–29

Z
ziggurats, 23
zooarchaeologist, 39